D0245061

Tough Topics

Moving House

Patricia J. Murphy

www.heinemann.co.uk/library

Visit our website to find out more information about Heinemann Library books.

To order:
- ☎ Phone 44 (0) 1865 888066
- 🖹 Send a fax to 44 (0)1865 314091
- 🖥 Visit the Heinemann Library Bookshop at www.heinemann.co.uk/library to browse our catalogue and order online.

First published in Great Britain by Heinemann Library, Halley Court, Jordan Hill, Oxford OX2 8EJ, part of Harcourt Education. Heinemann Library is a registered trademark of Harcourt Education Ltd.

© Harcourt Education Ltd 2008
The moral right of the proprietor has been asserted.

All rights reserved. No part of this publication may be reproduced, stored in a retrieval system, or transmitted in any form or by any means, electronic, mechanical, photocopying, recording, or otherwise, without either the prior written permission of the publishers or a licence permitting restricted copying in the United Kingdom issued by the Copyright Licensing Agency Ltd, 90 Tottenham Court Road, London W1T 4LP (www.cla.co.uk).

Editorial: Charlotte Guillain
Design: Richard Parker and Q2A Solutions
Picture Research: Erica Martin
Production: Duncan Gilbert

Originated by Chroma Graphics (Overseas) Pte. Ltd
Printed and bound in China by South China Printing Company

ISBN 978 0 431 90786 4
12 11 10 09 08
10 9 8 7 6 5 4 3 2 1

British Library Cataloguing in Publication Data
Murphy, Patricia J.,
Moving house - (Tough topics)
1. Moving, Household - Psychological aspects - Juvenile literature
155.9'3

A full catalogue record for this book is available from the British Library.

Acknowledgements
The author and publisher are grateful to the following for permission to reproduce copyright material:
© Corbis pp. 6 (Zave Smith), 22 (Tim Pannell), 5; © Getty Images pp. 11 (Taxi/Arthur Tilley), 12 (The Image Bank/Brooklyn Productions), 15 (Peter Dazeley), 17 (Photodisc), 19 (Gary Houlder), 23 (The Image Bank/Florian Franke), 29 (Digital Vision); © Masterfile pp. 4 (Michael Mahovlich), 8 (Jerzyworks), 9 (David Schmidt); © Photoedit pp. 7, 13 (David Young-Wolff), 20 (Michael Newman); © Photolibrary p. 26 (Purestock), 28 (Veer Incorporated - Fancy); © Photolibrary.com p. 21; © Punchstock pp. 10 (Chris Carroll), 18 (Uppercut Images/Robert Houser), 24 (Uppercut Images/Hill Creek Pictures), 25 (UpperCut Images), 16, 27; © Superstock p. 14 (Stockdisc)

Cover photograph of for sale sign reproduced with permission of © Corbis/image100.

Every effort has been made to contact copyright holders of any material reproduced in this book. Any omissions will be rectified in subsequent printings if notice is given to the publishers.

Disclaimer
All the Internet addresses (URLs) given in this book were valid at the time of going to press. However, due to the dynamic nature of the Internet, some addresses may have changed, or sites may have changed or ceased to exist since publication. While the author and publishers regret any inconvenience this may cause readers, no responsibility for any such changes can be accepted by either the author or publishers.

COVENTRY CITY LIBRARIES	
PETERS	01-Nov-07
333.33	£10.50
CEN	

Contents

Some words are shown in bold, **like this**. You can find out what they mean by looking in the Glossary.

Moving house

Things are always moving. Birds fly south for the winter. Other animals also **migrate**, going to a new home as the seasons change. People move from place to place too.

Some people move house many times in their lives. Each move brings new experiences—some happy and some difficult.

Why do people move house?

▲ Families often need a bigger home when new children are born.

People move house for different reasons. Someone in the family may have a new job in a different place. Some people may wish to buy bigger or smaller homes. Others may want to live closer to loved ones.

Other people might choose to move to a warmer **climate** or to see other parts of the world. Whatever the reason, moving can be hard because you leave behind special people and places.

▶Leaving people you love behind is hard.

How do people move house?

Some people move far away from their old home. Some move just a few streets away. Either way, you must take everything with you when you move.

Before moving, you have to pack all of your things into boxes. Next, you need to load these boxes into cars or large vans. Some people use a removal company to help them move.

Getting ready to move

◄ You might worry how you will feel in your new surroundings.

Moving can be exciting, but it can also be scary. You may wonder if you will like your new town, new home, and new school.

You can look up information on your new town at the library or on the **Internet**. You could also visit before you move and meet some people who live there.

▲ Talking about your new home with your family will help you get ready to move.

Saying goodbye

Before moving away, you may want to say goodbye to family members, friends, and familiar places in your **neighbourhood**. Your family may have a party to say goodbye.

▶It is hard to leave a special place behind.

You might also say goodbye to your home. You could walk from room to room and remember the good times that you had in them. You can take these **memories** with you when you leave.

Staying in touch

When people move, they usually give their new address and phone number to family and friends before they leave. They may also take pictures to remember them.

▲ A photo of your friends will help you feel better if you miss them.

It is important to stay in touch with friends and family after you move. Phone calls, letters, emails, and visits will help you stay in touch. This might make moving away less sad for everyone.

Moving day

Moving day is a busy day. Boxes and furniture are moved out of the old home and into the new one. It can take days or weeks to unpack and get everything into the right place.

▲ Moving heavy furniture is hard work.

▲ Unpacking can be fun if you do it together.

Moving can be exciting, but it is also tiring and **stressful**. People may argue and get upset more easily on moving day. It is normal for these things to happen.

How does it feel to move house?

Some children may be happy to move house. They might see moving as a new adventure. They may be excited about living in a new place, **neighbourhood**, and **community**.

▶It can be fun to get out and explore your new neighbourhood.

Many people might be sad or angry about moving away from family and friends. They may also be afraid they might not fit in or make new friends. Sometimes, people have a mixture of these feelings.

Moving in

When you arrive at your new home, everything you loaded into the cars and moving van has to be moved in. Then you have to unpack the boxes. Things will be all over the place!

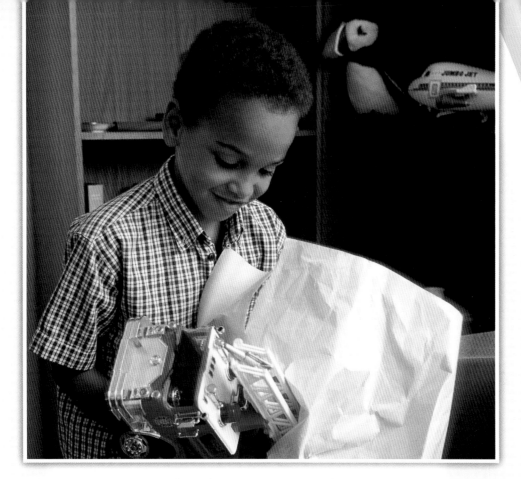

▲ It can be fun to unpack your favourite things.

Unpacking can be a happy time when you find places to put your things. It can also be upsetting when you cannot find things that you need. While you pack, it is a good idea to label your boxes so you know what is inside them.

New places

▲ Get a map of your new town to help you find your way around.

A new town has many new places to discover. These places may include new shops, parks, schools, libraries, museums, and **community** centres.

To find these places, you could walk or drive around town with an adult. You could go to the **town hall**, or **tourist information office** to ask questions or directions.

▲ Introduce yourself to neighbours and other people you meet.

Loneliness

Being in a new town can be **lonely**. Neighbours are strangers at first, and family and friends may feel far away. You may wonder when you will start to fit in.

▲ It is normal to miss the people and places you have left behind.

▲ If you feel lonely for a long time, share your feelings with a parent or trusted adult.

With a little time and effort, you will feel like a part of your new town and meet new friends. Try to look for good things in your new home and neighbourhood.

Making new friends

Making new friends is not always easy. Sometimes it takes hard work. Some people might not seem very friendly. Others might act like they do not need any new friends.

◄ It can be hard to tell if someone wants to be your friend.

▶Playing a sport is a great way to meet people.

To make friends, you have to be brave. You have to say hello and tell people your name. You could join a club or sign up for a team sport. Some of the people you meet might turn into friends.

Feeling at home

Once you have unpacked all the boxes and put things away, you will begin to feel comfortable in your new home. Soon your sad feelings will go away.

▲ It is normal to have sad feelings about moving.

▲ Family is what makes any place feel like home.

For most people, moving is a good experience. It teaches you how to handle change. Often, it can bring families closer together.

29

Moving tips

- Label all of your boxes with a marker. For example, label boxes for your clothes, books, and toys. This will make it easier to find things when you unpack.

- Pack a moving day bag. Put things like your toothbrush and favourite book in this bag and keep it with you on moving day. This way, you will have what you need before you are completely unpacked.

- Set up your room the way you want it as soon as you can. This will help you feel more at home.

- Take your time unpacking. Do not try to do it all at once. Take some breaks and spend time with your family. Your things will be there when you get back.

- Visit the town with your family and introduce yourself to your neighbours. Soon, your new town will feel like home.

Glossary

climate usual weather in a region or area

Internet computer network that links computers worldwide

lonely feeling alone

memories things you remember from your past

migrate change location seasonally from one area to another

neighbourhood area in a city or town where people live

stressful causing worry

tourist information centre place where visitors go to learn more about a place

town hall where a town's government offices are located

More books to read

Lucy's New House (First Experiences), Barbara Taylor Cook and Siobhan Dodds (School Speciality Publishing, 2002)

I Want That Room!: Moving House, Jen Green and Mike Gordon (Hodder Wayland, 2007)

Moving House (First Times), Rebecca Hunter (Evans Publishing, 2004)

Index